No Farther Than the End
of the Street

No Farther Than the End of the Street

neighborhood poems

by Benjamin Niespodziany

Okay Donkey Press

Published by Okay Donkey Press

Los Angeles, CA 90034

www.okaydonkeymag.com

First edition. November 2022.

ISBN: 978-1-7332441-8-3

Cover art: Raysa Fontana

For Ninche

Student: What's outside of Pleasantville?

Teacher: What? I don't understand.

Student: Outside of Pleasantville. What's at the end of Main Street?

Teacher: Oh, Mary Sue. You should know the answer to that. The end of Main Street is just the beginning again.

— *Pleasantville* (**1998**)

Truman: You can't get any farther away before you start coming back.

— *The Truman Show* (**1998**)

Table of Contents

I. Yardmouth

II. Baffling Scaffolding

III. The Flimsy Chimney

IV. Front Lawn Songs

V. Partial Architectures

I. Yardmouth

First Date

You bought a plot of land and you dug a hole.
You filled the hole with seasoned meat and cedar
and silk. You covered the hole and you waited. It
was supposed to take nine months, but I arrived
in seven. When I appeared I was grown and
vocal. You held me like a science finalist. The
floor plan was stamped to my chest.

Second Date

My heart dropped and you stepped on it. It wasn't your fault. I dusted off my crushed lump, my slowed blood, and held it in my weakening digits. You apologized. I apologized. Years later, we promised to name our first child by picking a name out of a vase.

Third Date

After we neighborhood kissed we moved in to
what we built and the sky died and we walked to
where your heart was buried and then walked to
where my heart was buried and you said you
could hear your heart beating before we arrived
and we dug for months and at once you held
yours and I held mine and at once you swallowed
yours and I swallowed mine and we promised to
one day return to where our hearts were once
buried, our home a cold distance, listen, the fog
in our mouths like ghosts.

Toe in the Snow Blower

I lose my toe in the snow blower and you run circles like a swirl. You look like a firetruck stuck in a lake. You dig through the snow blower and find a litter of kittens. You bring inside the litter of kittens and provide the kittens a home. I feed them seeds. You personalize their paper crowns. You reach farther into the snow blower and find a human skull. It's on display in our basement next to faded paintings of bees. Again, you reach into the snow blower and find my toe, but my toe has turned peach. Flat like a ring. You take a bite and spit the pit, but the pit is not my toe. "Drupe," you say, and chew again. "What?" I ask. "Peach," you repeat. "Pitch?" I ask. You spit more pits and still no toe. You wipe your mouth against the snow blower. The kittens are sleeping. The hum is their comfort. My toe is their dream.

Sage and Citrus

The candles arrived
on time so we
ordered more candles.

This went on
for years. A neighbor
we admired stopped

wearing her favorite sweater.
We both noticed
and wept.

Viral Try [1]

Come out and see, I'm donned in monstique...

I dressed in monster
truck tires

and rolled
down our neighborhood hill.

When a crowd did not form
and our neighbors still hid

you took note
of what we did not know.

Viral Try [2]

When the night was a golden bone...

I learned how to burn my hand without
screaming. You learned how to fit in a fish tank
and hold your breath. We phoned our neighbor
to come over and record us. We were close.

Viral Try [3]

On our balcony...

You wore a crown of candles. I lit them one by
one. On the balcony, our neighbor arrived and
placed his cassette player into a drained
aquarium. "The night sounds like black and
white," he said, "like the Sunday after next."
Our charcoal grill cooked a skinned squirrel.
None of us knew what to do when it was ready.
Our neighbor grew heavy, painted our nails
violet and left without saying goodbye. A car
crash happened four doors down – a van and a
chicken coop. We shook it away, prayed together
upon learning the vultures would not leave.
Words heard differently, bracelets the same.
Before turning in, we watched a neighbor in the
sky with hundreds of balloons pleading for a
hand.

Viral Try [4]

The hearing theater...

You were near completion eating a barbershop beacon atop the cedar in our backyard. I was filming. "What is the meaning," you asked our captive neighbors, "of the hearing theater?" Every single arm went up. One had to purchase a ticket if one wanted to talk.

You, You See, Everyone's Counting on We

Somewhere in our backyard, I'm singing atop a
stage shaped like your state. Every neighbor in
the crowd is a cow. Guitar strings sting my hands.
I look at the teleprompter for assistance. It tells
me now to bow. I bow and see you tying tight my
moon shoes. I'd love to hug you, you see, but I
have this decade-long song to sing.

Triple Lung

The lung in my backpack is in my backpack
because I need a third lung to breathe. This is
selfish of me, I know. My neighbor claims seas
breed whales that never stop swimming. Even
when they sleep. I'm opening my mouth. I'm
holding my air.

Whale in a Well

At the bottom
of our backyard
wishing well
there rests a baby whale
that I wished for.

It looks spellbound
like a mountain. I know
the baby whale
will grow and the well
will not. I'm trying my best

to build for it
a bucket. I'm wishing
in the well for help. The baby
whale calls are loud
and only I can hear them.

Can Heaven Call for Back-up?

From a cloud above, an angel and a piano fell onto our front lawn. Their stomachs both hosted broken strings. I organized my grief by buying a conductor tux. You set up a booth and I just stood there as the tragedy attracted a crowd. The flaps and the buttons. The hell of it all. Later that night, I cried as I dug, grunted as I buried the final bone then final key. It happened so fast, the dirt unearthed, the piano returned to the lawn. By morning, a garden had blossomed atop the angel's soft rot.

Dawn

You tuned the fallen piano that refused to hide. I stuffed it with flowers. You sat in your lawn chair, and you performed a long song. I ate eight petals. The piano cried. Each key was an injury. We would not bury her again. We wheeled the piano into the alley. It became overrun with ferns, vines, mice, twine. Rats, bats, raccoons. The dismantled piano reveled in its mutated nature. When it rained the fallen piano sang the loveliest of songs. We visited every Sunday and wore our best feathers. Church service without a wordy sermon. We watched the piano no longer in the sky act natural in its new environment. We tried to do the same.

Bloodletting

You were an angel created in a landfill. I measured your wingspan. We sat in our backyard and split a pitcher of sangria. You said the circus stole your identity some centuries ago. Wiped you off the grid and, in exchange, gave you rust-feathered flappers. Wings made of dog bones and flutes, lamp posts and foil.

As soon as you were able, you escaped the circus. I sliced more fruit. "I had to do so on foot," you said, a piece of chicken wire falling from your shoulder and onto the floor. "These don't fly." You were terrified of what the future might sculpt. The wings were connected to you in a way that they couldn't be removed unless you wanted to lose your arms.

Away from the circus, the wings stuck out like desert vending machines. You wore massive sweatshirts to job interviews, and no one called you back. You'd been considering odd assignments like throwing people down the stairs. We prepared more ideas on the bark of one of our trees. We act so haphazardly when we're promised anonymous wings.

"Years from now," you said, sculpting a bar of soap into a tiny home, "when I finally decide to jump and really test these wings, you'll be miles below, alone, laughing in the grass, certain I'm finally flying."

Refuel

You level
our backyard and lay
the tarmac.

Planes pay us
to land
and take off.

I sell dolls
dressed like flight
attendants and fighter pilots.

One doll is made of moon
light, another designed like
a pocket watch, another a horse.

I spend my lunch
breaks watching lovers pull apart
arms, bracelets, braids of hair.

A mother wraps her daughters
in strings of pink balloons,
popping loudly not quite home.

Everyone wants to feel
secure before curving
through the sky.

I hold up a doll, my favorite
doll, the one that looks
like an emergency landing.

Everyone is safe
but the plane
is in flames.

With this doll, the slide
has to be used. Everyone
wants to use the slide.

It's the most expensive doll
we offer and everyone
asks its price.

Yellow Helicopter

In our front lawn spins a helicopter. The pilot steps out with a clipboard and tells me to sign. His knuckles are tattooed Roman numerals beginning with 7 and ending at 14. "I didn't order this," I tell him, "I ordered a ring. A wedding ring. A tiny diamond wedding ring." He shows me the receipt. You're asleep in our home, dreaming like a boat.

II. Baffling Scaffolding

Costumes Encouraged

The weddings were plentiful.
We attended them all. Most

were in our backyard while others
less lustrous were held down the street.

In one, you were dressed as a pelican.
In another, a mother of sun.

I was the same. Always the sprained
ankle. The rainstick. The townhouse

caught in a crowd. Leather
penance regretted making sense.

After one wedding, we found ourselves
smelling the storm.

A praying pilot on our sidewalk.
A lost dog licking his boots.

The wedding planner

proclaimed it a disaster. The minister was sick
with liver failure. I, the groom, was in a tomb,
loose-lipped and blue. You, the bride, were lively
from adrenaline injections. The wedding was
broken, bleeding, sleeping on the altar. Even the
flower girl, Myrtle – age eight – was so overcome
with pain that she spit up clumps of petals she'd
called Eden. Even the deacon, who was not
invited, described the wedding as the opposite of
heaven. A stray cat passing through, pawing at
the platters, not understanding the frantic nature
of humans in dress.

Wedding Masks

We were supposed to get married on an island but instead we go into our basement. "I didn't know we had a basement," you say. You're supposed to have a veil, and I, polka dot loafers. In our basement, there's a clerk behind glass. "Did you bring ten dollars?" the clerk asks. "Yes," we tell her, "yes." We were supposed to get married on a cliff overlooking crashing waves. Under the glass we pass the ten dollars. It was supposed to be flowers, awnings, tides. The sweaty judge arrives. "My eleventh today," he shouts through a crackling speaker. We were supposed to get married next to groups of friends from everywhere. Instead, we are our own witnesses. You say I do, I say I do. We both do. It's official. We're married downstairs.

We walk up the steps and into the sunlight and see a neighbor across the street pushing a bus full of tourists. She's preaching. She's seething. She yells and she yells. Maybe she'll save them.

Tourism

The hunter visited our street two hours on foot
from her town. She removed her rifle when our
mailman sang. "I'm sorry," the hunter said,
putting her rifle away. "I thought you were a
wolf." She continued walking. From a neighbor
boy, the hunter bought a bouquet of daisies. She
paid in elk bone and locust. She explored the
flora's stability by trying to pry a fire hydrant.
She gripped a walking stick layered in bug spray
and claimed, "It gets tricky in a park with this
many trails." She sought a duck sanctuary or
some waterfalls but neither did our street offer.
She dashed over rock and gawked at the glass
that cascaded the sky. I continued to follow the
hunter no farther than the end of our street,
breathing heavily in my grizzly suit, just as she
had asked.

Chainsaw Neighbor

A neighbor with a chainsaw chainsawed the only tree in our front lawn. We asked our neighbor with the chainsaw why he was chainsawing the only tree in our front lawn. We did not request this service. He was sweating everywhere. A limousine drove by with a pine tree on top. Our neighbor with a chainsaw stopped chainsawing to watch.

A Matryoshka Picnic

You prepare us a picnic basket. Inside the picnic basket is a smaller picnic basket. Inside the smaller picnic basket is an even smaller picnic basket. This persists for some time until eventually we reach the smallest picnic basket where inside is a tiny lunch that never rots like the world it waits to leave.

In Our Backyard Garden

With a pitcher of water, I stood next to a neighbor
who had dying flowers for a face.

The flowers surrounded. They covered his skin.
I heard him breathing. He smelled

like a storm. A bee slept on one of his
struggling petals. From my pitcher I poured

a few drops on top of his head.
Another neighbor arrived. Just like the first,

she too had flowers for a face. Different
aromas and styles, but flowers nonetheless.

Her flowers were stronger. Brighter.
Not dying. Keeping more bees.

"Hi," she said to the neighbor.
"Hi," he replied. They both

looked at me, me without any flowers
for a face, me watering my many planted flowers

and together they said
nothing.

Spinning a Web Like a Veteran

You rolled up your sleeves like a prize fighter, so
this is what I called you. You misheard. You
thought I said prize spider. I tried to explain that
you were a boxer and not a bug, an abundance
of muscle, but it was awfully late: you were
already dangling in the corner nearly reaching
the ceiling.

A Mutual Duel

When you challenged the neighbor-hood mayor
to a bake off in our front lawn, I was coughing
wrongdoings in our backyard. The blood that
hung from my lips was, from a distance, divine. I
tried to paint the naked soil evergreen and failed.
I tried to match the palette and lost. You won the
gold, brought it into our home, beholden in your
grip as if the apple medallion was you.

Publicity Stunt

I wrote you a poem
called "Planet Earth."
It's a ghost
poem or maybe a poem

I ghost wrote. It's an
X-ray I pass around
the neighborhood.
It's what's happening

inside my torso. It's an anteater
clawing a tree trunk, leaping
to reach a termite nest
as the branches catch fire.

When I pass around the ghost
poem, I make sure to say, "A camera crew
is filming my internal concerns, but
we're unsure of the channel."

I start again: I wrote you this ghost poem.
It's called "Planet Earth."
It's just an X-ray. It's something
meant to connect. I start again:

we're all a little confused
and I don't understand why
you laughed or why
you're still laughing.

The Harmless Gardener

We could no longer afford our gardener. I asked
him over to talk. He arrived hanging onto his
cane. I looked and his cane became a sword. I
looked again, his sword was a mailbox. The flag
was raised. I opened the door. Out poured
letters. Some wet with rain. Now his mailbox was
a shovel. New garden shears, sharp. With them,
he dug up our front lawn, planted tree seeds,
marigolds. Made floral our home. It was then we
knew we could spend a little extra. It was then
we three fell gently asleep.

Long Distance Relationship

I found pound
cake in my mouth.

Perfectly baked,
resting on my tongue.

Whenever I removed
a slice, another took its place.

"Dear?" I said
to you, sounding mumbly

like I had
pound cake in my mouth.

The cakes were overtaking
the kitchen.

You exhaled from the other room.
"Can you come here?" I asked.

I started sweating. The cakes continued.
Our neighbors knocked and noticed

the cakes escaping
my mouth. We'd worked so hard

to not be odd. "What is it?" you
finally said, still within

the other room, grooming
our newborn stork.

Gender Reveal Party

Our neighbors huddled around us as I loaded the flare gun and fired into the sky. Your plump stomach was the size of a ripe cantaloupe. Boys and girls used binoculars and telescopes, voted blue or pink and hoped with their throats. "We're so proud of you two," said the adults. "We can't wait to meet the new addition." The flare bared a green emission that illuminated the sky. Green like game show slime, green like tree teeth. Our neighbors looked down at me crouching, you beside me, loading another flare. One neighbor mumbled, "What the hell?" Another shouted, "Well, what does green mean? Is it a boy or not?"

Second Gender Reveal Party

You opened a golden box. Out crawled a sloth holding a doll. You opened another box: a miniature horse and a miniature buggy. A track of AstroTurf. Another box of frosty moss with a top that did not open. Neighbors watched as if under a velvet spell. Standing away from the boxes – a box of stopwatches, a box of dog bones – you took a bag of sand, and you took a jug of water and together you began to mix. "The thick of it," said a neighbor, his gaze returned to the turf.

III. The Flimsy Chimney

Spectacles

I watched you eat our home
from our front lawn.
It took you eight weeks.

Once you were done, you birthed
a nursery. A tiny highway.
A street our street called Home.

I watched you mend meadows.
I watched you frame windows.
"They're my children," you said.

It was out of my hands. My lawn
chair broken. I sewed another.
You rose so slowly to bend.

Grief

You chose
the flowers
without petals.
The vase
with
murky waves.
You started
to explain
and then
stopped.

Quick Fix

It's late.
You're meditating.

I'm turning
into glass.

You're late.
I'm meditating.

You've made famous
our home.

I'm late.
Delayed meditating.

I'm awakening
the sculpt.

You're eating the moon.
You're wetting your feathers.

We'll never have enough
fruit for forever.

The weather is a metaphor
dreams refuse to explain.

We're scratching
our throats.

Our home once had a ring.
We sing to its myth.

Individual Design

We left behind our owls to attend a neighbor's dinner.

"The owls will be fine," you said on the walk, "we're just going down the street." You held a glow-in-the-dark star chart. I flipped through pictures of the owls. You adjusted my tie: a tie spotted and speckled in freckled owl eyes.

"They'll be fine," you said again. I could still see our place in the distance, the dimly lit windows, the owls now alone.

Up ahead, a school bus was unloading a group of children, each one skilled at finding their short way home.

Neighbor

You witnessed her death on our street. Your feet
were in the street, but your body was in the lawn.
I was inside our home, crouched like a cloud.
"Now he's a widow," you said, pointing to the
grieving husband across the street as he sleepily
watched his wife being carted away. The next
day, we went to the funeral in their backyard.
Everyone was there, even the dead wife. She was
floating over her coffin like some type of goblin
we wanted to trust. An antelope leaned against
their fence. After the funeral, authorities ended
up taking your mug shot. Now you cough
without a bonnet. Now you claw at the attic's
moon. Too soon, the body was gone and we were
back to talking about lawn darts and starter
homes. I was alone. You were alone. We held
hands.

You're Your Twin's Twin

On our tenth wedding
anniversary
you informed me
you're a twin.
We waited
in our front lawn
to meet her
and I looked
for someone
identical to you,
someone with
the same hands
as you,
same stance,
a picnic basket
of clasps and straps,
but I saw no staples.
I saw no labels. I went inside
and you did not.
You found teeth
and glued teeth
onto your teeth.

Coffin Gin

I was paid to paint the arms of strangers. You
soaked your coat in the concept of the dead.
Together, we slept like bed spring kingpins,
drawing with chalk on our roof. Used shoes in a
box in a locked closet. The denizens spending
time with the pigs.

One Corner of the War

A beast with one long arm and one normal arm leveled the forest behind our home. We walked when the clouds cleared and slept in what was left of the world. When our eyes reopened, we were back inside our home beneath a table that once breathed as tree. Sitting around the table was a family of three, unknown, muddling grovels of politics. You wiped the sleep from my eyes. You wiped the leaves from my feet. You removed the pen from my breast pocket, and you wrote our names on the floor. Through it all the family above us continued to eat the last living animal. Casual, whole.

Box Empty

Beneath our bed, I fold myself slowly into the shoebox of my favorite things. Pictures of rivers I once dreamed. Lakes I once drank. Bulldozer bolts. The seaweed spleen of a whale shark. I hold my smile like a serpent squeeze. You close the door and together we wait. Our fists as soft as cloth.

Blank Canvas

From night to morning, we read bedtime stories.
You bite your finger until you reach the bone.
You look outside our window as the sun begins
to rise. I call our empty home the Blank Canvas.
You call it many things. The Box Empty. The
Box Lost. I relax my forehead. I braid your hair.
Outside our Blank Canvas, I hear the hearts of
charged men. Torches lit. The front door is
kicked open. I can smell their fire, can hear their
tongues. You're still looking out our window. You
count something on your fingers. I'm not sure
what. The teeter-totter on our roof jiggles with
the wind.

When the War Formed

When the war formed in our corner of the room
we moved to another corner of the room. "We're
safe here," we said to each other, eyeing the
corner with the war. When the war found us in
our new corner we stepped out of the window
and took to the roof. We could hear the war
below us, fighting and writhing, such muffled
exhaust. "We're safe here," we said to each other
again, our neighbors' screams ringing with pleas.

Mid-Home Invasion

Out fell my gold tooth. A neighbor found my gold tooth and sold my gold tooth to a goldsmith down the street. The goldsmith discovered my gold tooth hollow and cracked it open with a spoon. Inside, he found a rolled-up scroll in an old language, another tongue, a prayer the goldsmith's own grandmother used to sing. "But how?" the goldsmith whispered. The paper was made of mulberry. The ink of squid and rain.

A Dance with Balance [1]

The gold vultures

in our backyard

continue swimming closer

and in a cloud nearby

some guy disguised as God

either can't stop coughing

or really

doesn't want to.

A Dance with Balance [2]

Under our home

there floats a ghost.

I know the ghost

doesn't know us

and I know we don't know

the ghost

but our intertwined lullabies

are trying to scream.

IV. Front Lawn Songs

Moth Lungs

At one of our costume parties, you dressed
like a butterfly and I like a moth.

butterflies usually rest with their wings closed
while moths rest with their wings open

I acted like a jet plane like old times. You stood
on the roof and looked at our pond.

butterflies have long thin antennas
while moths have shorter feathery antennas

When you hugged me, my scales
smothered you in dust. You loved it.

butterflies generally gather food during the day
while moths seem to feed more at night

"I can't sleep," I said, ten minutes
past six. You storm-snored like a bullfrog.

most moths make a silky cocoon
while butterflies make a shiny chrysalis

When our costume party was over and we sobered
up, I returned to normal and you flew away.

You moved

on. I bought the magic carpet
from your half of our half-
off yard sale
and now it doesn't work.

I went to return the magic carpet, but you moved
on. "To what part of our street?" I asked my new
roommates. "To Peru," they said, and persuaded me
to help unpack their boxes.
Socks and bottle caps. Button-downs and clown shoes.

"Do you have any magic carpets?" I asked
my new roommates but my new roommates
too were gone.

A Picnic [1]

My Off-the-Market Magic Carpet

I practiced with my magic carpet in our front lawn and looked like I was picnicking alone. I was waiting for its eyes to open, and when they did not, it felt like slowly sewing shut the sky.

A Picnic [2]

<u>A Wilted Mistletoe is Known to Kill its Tree</u>

Most of our mistletoe died. I packed the rest.
You called me from the other side of the world
and said you were still waiting for the year to
begin. "I'm not in the future like you," you said
to me, and I told you I don't own a clock.

A Picnic [3]

<u>You Left Your Drained Aquarium in Our Front Lawn</u>

When you sang, I half-sang micro-seconds
behind you, like an echo, like a crowd, like a vow.

After

After many months, I open your safe. Inside, I find a turkey. I reach into the turkey and I find a smaller safe. I try to open the smaller safe but the smaller safe is too small. I crawl around our home looking for clues. You won't pick up your phone. It's early and yet we're almost dead.

House Visit

I broke my leg. Snapped it like a branch. My limb a scrambled puzzle. "Your bone," the doctor said, "it's not a bone. It's not a bone," he said. "It's a boat. A Viking ship," he said. "A clinker build, I think, maybe caravel. Whatever you did," he said, "it shattered. Your ship shattered." He showed me the X-ray. He showed me the broken pieces. The pulpit and the boom. The wheel and the keel. They floated through my blood like clumps of hair. "To repair will take forever," he said. "Indeed, you need sealant. A new crew. Your ship is ruined." I felt the slowing heartbeat of my captain collapsing onto his knife.

House Call

My yoga instructor smells like velvet. "Address me as Toucan," she demands. I forget her name and call her Parakeet, Cockatiel, Pelican. "Ostrich?" I ask and think Flamingo. She points to her shirt that reads: *This is a ceremony. Only hum. If one must speak, be it whisper. A hush. We rest our wings, we breathe.* My leg does not get better. Toucan uncans oils. With her eyes, she tells me to bend and rest, to kill my vultures, to wound my inner crow. Mimic a finch. As the rainforest pours through her phone, she loans me a bird mask. It falls off mid-form. It hurts to stretch and hold. Toucan wears a mask that's more expensive than mine. It sits tight, the price tag dancing on the side. Her eyes of fine smoke. I try to remember her name after I call her Canary. Her owl sound marks the closing of the session. I knock over her rainstick. She gathers her mat.

The Silence That Finds Us

You can't
take my call. You're busy

making volcanoes
out of swamp products

and ketchup packets.
You call me back

weeks later and I can't
reach the phone

from my yoga position.
I let it go

to voicemail and you mention
how you're going to be

taking a trip soon.
You promise to call once

the plane lands. A few months pass
and I get a call from you

half past midnight.
You're still on the flight.

You explain flaps
and drag and wind

currents. I'm curling my hair
in our bathroom. I'm splashing

my feet in the tub.
I have you

on speakerphone
alone in our home.

I fall asleep listening
to your engine roar

like a twister
in a blender. I call you

one year later
but you're on a horse

track with maps and binoculars.
"An investment opportunity,"

you say. You promise
to call back once

the deal is done.
You tell me how

a horse's mouth
takes up more space

than its brain, how
horses have the largest

eyes of any
land mammal.

"I once heard horses
can't vomit,"

I say, but you
hang up

the phone.
I hear beeps

and then for years
I hear nothing.

You call the next
decade when we're both available.

All this free time to talk
now and nothing to say.

Rat Hands
or, Lurid Sky

When you left
you left
behind your
rat hands.

Dried in a tiny jar
you wore
around your neck.

"A conversation
starter," you told me
on our eighth
or ninth date.

On the many walks
up and down our street,
I used to hate neighbors
asking about your
rat hands.

When we
were fighting,
when it got bad,
a neighbor interrupted
and asked. "Not now,"
you said. When he

persisted, I said the same.
When he persisted, you told him
they were not rat hands.
"They're
squirrel claws," you said.

He had many
questions. We were
failing. I hurried
down the street.

Organizing My Books According to Page Number Reached

I'm eating
your left behind items:
your nightgown, your lawn
mower, your snow blower, your
eels. I'm blending
your sweaters.
I'm drinking
them down.

Blue

In the lake
in our backyard, I feed a whale
a cupcake.
It thanks me and escapes
into the blue. More lucid
than usual.
More lightning, more god.
All thanks
to the cupcake.
My cupcake. Sometimes
it's impossible
not to cry.

Unwander

No longer called
to wander
I kept

to my backyard
marrying and divorcing
two earthworms

living in
a split
tennis ball.

They claimed it
their oasis.
Who was I

to disrupt
such
glory days?

Our street's funeral
home made a note
for more bulbs.

The night
was cold, young,
still just a child.

A New Pair of Gloves

At first, I was the only one who noticed the noise.
My ear nearby. So cautiously lost in ivy was an
ivory tub. Beneath leaf and tree moss. It asked
to be unearthed. I positioned it with bricks. I
cleaned it and polished it and watered it and
rinsed. A crowd of neighborhood familiars
began to form. Curious swarms exhaling
question marks about the tub. What does the tub
say? What does the tub tell? Before long, I was
selling hats. Bathmats. Sponges. Strong sewn
statements like I Might Need a Scrub®, or I Do
Believe in Bathing Daily©. Often there was a
line for the tub. A line to step inside. To take
pictures from within. I helped every balancing
hand, every neighbor in need of a crutch. Some
said the gutter spoke deeply. Some said the drain
was ours.

A Picnic [4]

A Place to Practice Magic

I built a shed
in the middle
of our backyard. It's where
I keep my top hats,
my swords, a tiny
stool upon which
I practice the magic
of answering a knock.

Seamstress

door number [1]

I open the door
and our seamstress is spinning
on the porch.

She's wearing the feathers
of four dead parrots, they line her
black topstitched hat.

She's holding
a buttonhole embroidered
in tack.

She peels back
her hat and reveals
another, fifth parrot

balancing on her head
in a tiny cage.
The fifth parrot

is alive, relaxed
like a man
in a catapult.

The Pair of Married Mimes
door number [2]

A pair of married mimes stood outside our front door
ready to make eye contact.

They were from the neighborhood. Good people
with silent smiles. "How long have you been out here?"

I asked, opening the door. The wife had a clock
around her neck the size of a steering wheel.

She didn't answer. The husband clipped invisible
flowers with his fingers.

"You could have just knocked," I said. They both laughed
quietly like swallowing bees.

I handed the husband the wallet I had found on the sidewalk
during last week's snowstorm.

They were grateful for this deed. I could tell
by the way their eyes rained. It pained me

to watch them walk away holding hands, pointing
at the moon like it knew what to say.

The Parish

door number [3]

The Parish kicked down our door, invaded our kitchen, knocked over my favorite vase. Startled, I spilled a bowl of oatmeal on my suit. The Parish flipped my mattress, dug around our backyard. The Parish leapt over mouse traps in our basement and tripped over the lawn chairs in our garage. "We are fine churchgoing people," the Parish whispered upon entering every room. "Do you know where our church might be?" I told the Parish it was mistaken. "This is a home," I said. The Parish continued to look for an altar. "Might it be in the pantry?" the Parish asked. The Parish spooned through my oatmeal in search of a church. "Where is the blood?" the Parish asked, walking out back and checking the shed. "We are fine churchgoing people," the Parish said, and proceeded to hunt forever.

You You You

You taught a junkyard
to speak, winked
at the moon when it started
to move. You read the riot
act and overreacted halfway
through the introduction,
corrupted a dozen
trapeze artists to start
a diet of light tightrope. You wrote
home with your tears, misquoted
the world's first words. You
dealt me diamonds in a game
I never understood. You called you
and cried over you and comforted
you in the you of the storm. You prayed
to make it home safely. You broke
your hands and mailed
me the X-rays, attaching
a homesick note that read,
"Aren't these our wings?"

I Wipe My Eyes with My Sleeve

door number [4]

I spin in my swivel chair and
glare at the stereo's grief.

Seventy-four million mornings in a row
I eat alone until, again, you knock.

V. Partial Architectures

Making Friends

Setting the metronome
on its side, you ironed
the bed sheets.

"This is not
a bad thing,"
you said to me.

You ironed and I washed
and together we
waited for our new guests.

"This is not a bad thing
at all," I agreed,
fumbling with a record

to soundtrack the backdrop.
Something jazzy, something
sad.

Floral Shorts

door number [5]

He's knocking on our door and holding a load of roses. I let him step inside.

"I'm sorry," he says. He takes off his shoes and he tries on mine.

"I have to say," I say.
"Last May," he says.
"Last May?" I say.
"I was your waiter," he says.
"You were my waiter?" I say.
"I was your waiter down the street."

I had nothing to say.

"You were not mean-spirited, but you were indeed spirited."

He laughs. I laugh.

"But I thought," I say, and my thought I do not finish.

A cool breeze opens our home's windows. Same shade, same shape.

His wife knocks on our front door with more flowers. You step in from the garage with even more flowers, the same as the ones in the vase. Flowers in the wife's pockets. Flowers in the wife's hair. Our home houses flowers it didn't house the day before. None of us talk about how the flowers we hold are struggling so subtly to breathe.

82

Weather Forecast

"It's 53," you say. I point to the sweater
I bought down the street.

You're wearing a coat without arms.
"It will be 60 soon," you say.

The rats in our neighbors' trash
do not run when we pass them.

My sweater is coming apart.
We have to tarp our neighbors' chairs

while they're on vacation. They're paying us
in trust. Our wall has been leaking

for three years. Your tea is flavored like coffee.
My coffee is flavored like coffee.

No, it is not yet lunch. Yes, we are making a day
out of power washing the flood

so that we can sit with the sun when the sun
wants to scream. When it decides

it's time. "Soon," you say, again,
"it will again be 60 soon."

You, the Comic
or, Our Backyard Set

You choked on a bone
near the end of your set
and died. I and all our neighbors
laughed at first
but when we
understood, we stopped.
Most walked home.

That night, all of us
who were at the show
ate slower, smaller bites.
We sat in front of our static
televisions and like mannequins
we stared like air.

One fan named Jan, devout
from the crowd, attended your funeral
to deliver your final punchline.
Jan loved you. She wanted to help.
She wanted to laugh again.
We all did.

The hurdle on the field
leans sleepily to the left. The hurdle
on the field
is impossible to clear.

It Begins Again with Cicada Skin

Following your own death, you assemble a chair out of cicada skins and sit in our front lawn. A blimp coughs clouds. I am your spouse. I stand next to you in a coat made of stones. Down the street, a mother looks for her daughter. Both are lost. We cannot hear the neighbor playing piano a few houses down. When his silent song is complete, he winks at us, then goes inside to live.

Viral Try [5]

Livestream...

You film me swallowing my eyes. We've been talking about it for years. You use your new camera. Many tune in. Pay money to number the code, to observe me on the couch with my ounce bag of slime. We removed my eyes two nights prior and I haven't eaten since. The numbers are still rolling in. The live chat is rancid. Some bait, some pray. The money will be enough. You don't say much but the fine-with-quiet we've become.

She'll Come to Your Home, She'll Name All Your Rats

Every rat
in our attic
you've named.

Morton, Cortland,
Gordon, Dan.

We don't talk
about your past
rat hands.

We're cordial.
I'm eyeless, not asking
about the smell.
You feed me the tails.

You feed the rats
scraps of pizza and beef.
Chocolate, pieces of geese.

When the rats die,
their bones you throw
into my cold soup.

I can tell by their moonlight
tramples the rats
have exceeded one hundred.

Our neighbors
murmur said septic. I learn to not
bring it up.

Don't Let in More Rats

I sent a letter to the weather department and
they sent me back a batch of clouds. Our home
is already too small. My day is otherwise clear.
I'll be here. The key sleeps inside the lawn.

My Eyes, My Dear

I arrived at home with new eyes.
You were reading the paper.

I opened wide
and showed you my new blues.

"Those aren't new," you said,
returning to the paper. You were reading

a story about our neighbor who crashed
his bike into a fence lined with barbed wire.

Sergeants and surgeons were trying
to pull him apart and bring him

back together. "I promise you,"
I said, "these eyes are new."

I again showed you the blues, showed you
the reccipt. One receipt for each. Such expensive eyes.

"You've always had blue eyes," you said,
cutting out the news article

and hanging it on our fridge.
It was all we had. "I used to

have green eyes," I said. "I swallowed them."
You looked at me again

and again said, "No."
You walked to the bathroom

and counted the cracks in the tub.
Which one, you wondered, will uncover the flood?

Empty Canvas, Yellow Sky

or, The Very First Rain

I hurry around our backyard and cannot find
you. "You're late," you say, disguised like a tree.
I say nothing. "No matter," you continue. "It's
growing damp outside. From the sky. Have you
ever seen such a thing?" We break character and
look up. "What is it," I ask, "one brings to a very
first rain?" The grey clouds cry like roadside
assistance. We trade bags and sit a few yards
apart, watching as our world dampens then
grows.

Thursday

The rain clears its throat. I'm inside. I clear my throat. My throat turns to rain. The rain paints our windows. I try to decipher the words, but the words are weightless. My supplies are ghosts. On the other side of the street, two older neighbors in a swing sing a song about command. I try to dance along and when I can't, I dance it off.

Homework

The phone rings. It's the price of the people. It's the weatherman. It's God sobbing. I call for help and help does not call back. I fumble with the phone until the phone is not a phone and the phone is a bone of rain. The man in charge of my department is outside my front door. It's pouring. I adore him. He's dunking his cigarette in mud.

Moving Heavy Objects Across the Front Lawn

Can you bring in my box? It's raining. It's a granite anvil.
It's a what?
It's a weighted anchor.
It's shaped like a tooth.
It's a what?
It's a two-ton cedar slab. Sculpted to resemble our home.
It's a what?
It's an internal system for our newly refurbished kitchen.
It will help us do the dishes.
It's a what?
It's a dozen, no, wait, it's one hundred bowling balls
we'll someday use to line our walls.
It's a what?
It's a long coffin with room for both of us
to comfortably scrunch in, nail shut, and dream.

Whale Fables

All of my whales
are at the bottom
of wells or in lakes.
Places they
shouldn't be.
I'm with a whale
in our backyard right now.
Our neighbor is digging
a grave for his child's
pony. It's the only story
I know how to tell. The whale
says rain is better
than the ocean floor.
When it dies, it will open
its mouth, a shed
for us to vent.

White Ride

Our neighbor bought a white car and painted it red then again back to white. He sold them on the side. He amassed a fortune. During all of this, I was climbing our tree. He was frequently leaving, booking dinners all around town. His mask was half burlap and half gold. He saw me in the tree. Said he would cut me a deal. Said he would steal me a few. I watched him drive off often. Sometimes from our window, sometimes from our tree. He needed someone like me to look after him. I knew it. I noticed it and I knew it.

My neighbor invites me over to his home.

It's late. It's raining drainpipes. I walk across our front lawn. I walk across his front lawn. It's raining steak knives. I knock on his door. His wife answers. It's raining cat furs. She says he's in his barn. I knock on his barn. It's raining live Clydesdales. He opens the barn and lowers his shoulders. He's wearing a welding mask and a hazmat suit. It's raining roosters and hens. I say I'm sorry about the pony. He says he's too busy for company. I hear something growl within the border of his shadow. He shuts the door closed. His wife sees it all from their window. It's raining stained glass. I turn around and head home. His wife holds a tray of cheesecake squares for me to take with me. I walk over and extend my hand. She smiles. She understands. It's raining tin cans.

Melancholic Smell

Rain drains through our home. It covers the floors. You sit knitting a sweater. I'm in the kitchen kicking griddles and skillets. The rain reaches our ankles. An eel ignores our shoes. You keep knitting sweaters, I keep kicking griddles. "This will be the most lovely sweater," you say. It stretches past your knees and breathes into the water. "This will be the most delicious dinner," I say, kicking more skillets. The rainwater is now at our waists. The power has been out for days. Our flickering candles will soon know smoke. Outside, swimming above our front lawn, the patient crocodile knows not to knock.

The Stopwatch's Opposite

You held me how a giant might lullaby a
lightbulb. Outside the rain was a blanket you
called a chancre sore, and I called a wallet.
"Why," you asked, "does neither of us know how
to knit?" I shivered downward my tears. I held
to you our many sweaters, sweaters we'd built,
sweaters we'd never wear. I lifted your thin digits
wrapped in strands of thread and I pointed to
the pins in your teeth, and I pointed to the
scissors at your feet and yes you watched me like
a tongue watches a door and yes, the walls
dampened and still the harder it rained.

Wet Castle

The street floods.
I paint our canoe.

The water holds
floating shoes, hub

caps, gas cans. When
the water reaches our

window we open and
climb outside

and paddle down the block.
People are smoking

cigarettes on their roofs.
They wave like we're heroes.

We approach the tallest cow
we've ever seen. It's so tall

that its head is out
of the water like a telescope

hoping for stars. I've heard the loveliest
low that was the low from that cow.

The water rises as we pass
cow head island

and everything breaks my heart.

You All Along

You pull back the black curtain and I'm again on
stage in our new backyard, shaking. I'm always
so nervous. I'm drawing a claw on the side of a
box. It helps. You're the only one in the crowd,
writing on a napkin how to sound out my name.
Our name. There's a Z somewhere in the
middle. It's a trip.

Cast and Credits, in Order of Appearance:

"First Date" (originally titled "Origin Myth"), "One Corner of the War," and "After You Left" first appeared in *Wigleaf* and were nominated for *Best Microfiction*. Thank you.

"Third Date" and "The Stopwatch's Opposite" were both written after reading many wonderful Sasha Fletcher love poems. Thank you.

"Toe in the Snow Blower" was the first poem I read in front of a crowd. It was for *RHINO Poetry*'s Open Mic Night at AWP 2019 in Portland, where I first met poets Rick Bursky, Shivani Mehta, and C.T. Salazar. Thank you.

"Viral Try [3]" (originally titled "Balcony") first appeared in *Jet Fuel Review*. Thank you.

"Viral Try [4]: The Hearing Theater" takes its title by combining Leonora Carrington's novel *The Hearing Trumpet* and Russell Edson's collection *The Clam Theater*. Thank you.

"Bloodletting" (originally titled "While Drinking Sangria") first appeared in *Fairy Tale Review*. Thank you.

"Refuel" (originally titled "At the Airport Kiosk") first appeared in *Okay Donkey*. Thank you.

"Wedding Masks" and "Floral Shorts" both began in a *Bending Genres* weekend workshop led by Bud Smith. Thank you.

"Tourism" (originally titled "Chicago, a National Park") first appeared in *decomP*. Thank you.

"Chainsaw Neighbor" was written after reading Giacomo Pope's collection *Chainsaw Poems & Other Poems*. Thank you.

"Publicity Stunt" (originally titled "Planet Earth is a Publicity Stunt") first appeared in *The Operating System*. Thank you.

"Long Distance Relationship" first appeared in *The Indianapolis Review*'s Poets are Funny issue. Thank you.

"Gender Reveal Party" first appeared in *Paper Darts*. Thank you.

"Box Empty" and "Blank Canvas" used to be one combined poem and started as part of a self-induced prompt in conversation with Sabrina Orah Mark's poem "Box Three, Spool Five." Thank you.

"When the War Formed" first appeared in *Back Patio Press*. Thank you.

"Moth Lungs" features lines in italics taken from sciencebob.com's article on moths versus butterflies. Thank you.

"House Call" (originally titled "Hummingbird Bouquet") first appeared in *Meow Meow Pow Pow*. Thank you.

"The Silence That Finds Us" (originally titled "Call Collect") first appeared in *Peach Mag* and was nominated for a Pushcart Prize. Thank you.

"A New Pair of Gloves" (originally titled "Tub Gloves, Always New") first appeared in *Guesthouse* and is in direct conversation with "Outhouse" by Evan Nicholls, a poem that features a laughing bathroom. Thank you.

"The Pair of Married Mimes" first appeared in *Pithead Chapel.* Thank you.

"The Parish" first appeared in *Jellyfish Review.* Thank you.

"You You You" first appeared in *Pidgeonholes.* Thank you.

"You, the Comic" (originally titled "The Stand-up Comic") first appeared in *Fence.* Thank you.

"My Eyes, My Dear" began as a Russell Edson imitation poem. Thank you.

"Homework" first appeared in *the lickety ~ split.* Thank you.

"White Ride" (originally titled "White Ferrari") first appeared in *elsewhere.* Thank you.

"My neighbor invites me over to his home" (originally titled "You Invite Me") first appeared in *The Spectacle.* Thank you.

"Melancholic Smell", in particular its title, takes its language from earthbuddies.net, "5 Facts About Rain." Thank you.

Thank you to Michael Bazzett, Mikko Harvey, Evan Nicholls, C.T. Salazar, Zachary Schomburg, and Evan Williams for providing thoughtful feedback and insight and for looking so closely at this manuscript in its earlier forms.

Thank you to Matthew Olzmann for prompting me to "start with a joke, end with a prayer" in his interview on [neonpajamas]. I often approach the blank page with that line in my head.

Lastly, all of these poems are for and after and in conversation with and caricatures of my relationship with my spouse and my partner and my love Nina. These isolated domestic weird ones are all for you, Jim. Thank you, thank you, thank you.

Thank you.

About the Author

Benjamin Niespodziany's work has appeared in *Cheap Pop*, *Fence*, *Fairy Tale Review*, *Gone Lawn*, *Hobart*, *Wigleaf*, and various others. Along with being featured in the *Wigleaf* Top 50, his writing has been nominated for the Pushcart Prize, Best of the Net, and *Best Microfiction*. His debut chapbook *The Northerners* was released in 2021 by above/ground press and his second chapbook *Pickpocket the Big Top* was released in May 2022 by Dark Hour Books. *No Farther Than the End of the Street* is his debut full-length poetry collection. You can find out more at neonpajamas.com.

A Note from the Neighborhood Watch:

Thank you
for making
the rounds.

Now,

Won't you
please clean up
your clouds?

CPSIA information can be obtained
at www.ICGtesting.com
Printed in the USA
LVHW031649021222
734473LV00003B/520

9 781733 244183